Straight Talk About Living With A Severe Mental Illness

Darrell E. Herrmann

First Edition

13 November 2019

ISBN: 9781707189779

DEDICATION

Dedicated with great gratitude to those mental health professionals who take the time and effort to educate their patients about their illnesses and how to live with them.

Contents

ACKNOWLEDGMENTS

I would like to acknowledge the great support of my wife Kristen, and all the members of my treatment team. I would also like to acknowledge the people who have been in my hospital groups over the years for asking me challenging questions. It is through those questions that I learned what issues and information are of most concern and most needed by those suffering from severe mental illness.

I would also like to thank Roberta "Bobbie" McCord for providing the cover art for this book.

My Background and Story

In 1984, I was a captain in the United States Army. My specialties were field artillery and nuclear weapons. I began to believe that I had been drugged with an experimental drug as part of a secret conspiracy to produce super soldiers. I believed that I was having a bad reaction to this experimental drug and that this was why I couldn't sleep, couldn't cope with my work, and, in general, was not coping well with anything. Because I thought I had been drugged and was having bad side effects from it, I decided to go to the army hospital and ask them for help with this. They quickly realized that I was becoming delusional and psychotic. I wound up on a military psychiatric ward.

At that point, it was obvious that I needed to make a career change, as nuclear weapons and psychosis just don't go together very well. I decided to try to go back to college and become a computer programmer. At that time, no one knew if I could do that, not me and not the doctors, but that was what I wanted to do. In January of 1985, I started studying full time for my computer science degree. In December of 1986, I graduated and completed my degree. In January of 1987, I began working full time as a professional computer programmer. I did that successfully for almost 18 years until November of 2004 when the stress finally became too much for me and I went on disability.

In April of 1995, I relocated to Columbus, Ohio for a new job. In July of 1997, I bought my first PC and got onto the internet. I got involved with a schizophrenia support website, which was a godsend for me. For the first time since becoming mentally ill, I was able to talk to someone outside a psychiatric ward who had schizophrenia. When you are walking down the street, people do not have a sign on them saying "I have schizophrenia," so you don't know when you meet someone who has schizophrenia. If they do have schizophrenia, they aren't likely to tell you for the same reason you wouldn't tell them. At the website, we could talk openly about what worked and didn't work in treating our illness and give each other tips and tricks on how to live better with the illness. Then in 2001, I found a support group here in Columbus for my illness. It was the same as the website, except that now I was meeting people face-to-face and in person. We could go out to lunch together, or take in a movie together, or have a group picnic in the park.

In late 2002, Riverside Hospital approached the support group about having members talk on their psychiatric ward about living with a mental illness. I and some other members volunteered to do this. In January of 2003, we began doing groups on the Riverside psychiatric unit. After a couple of months, everyone had stopped doing these groups except me and Kay N. I found this volunteer work very rewarding as did Kay N. We both enjoyed helping others learn to live with their diagnosis. Kay N. worked with me for several years at Riverside. After I went on disability in 2004, I approached Mental Health America of Franklin County, who sponsored the community group and the hospital work as well, about expanding my volunteer job to other hospitals in Columbus. With their help I expanded to several other hospitals in the community. As of this writing, I am doing 7 groups per week at various hospitals here in Columbus. Over the last 10 years, I have spoken to more than 30,000 people in these hospital groups.

In return for all the volunteer work I was doing for the support group and my other efforts to improve the treatment of the mentally ill in Columbus, the executive director of Mental Health America of Franklin County nominated me for a Jefferson Award in 2007. I was one of five people from Central Ohio to receive a Jefferson Award in 2007. As part of the publicity for this award, an article about me was published in the *Columbus Dispatch*, as well as a 3-minute TV spot on me and my work. My winning the Jefferson award appeared as part of television newscasts several times during the month of April. I have also won numerous other awards for my volunteer work, but this is the most prestigious.

In 2007, a very special woman attended several of my hospital groups while she was a patient. She decided to come to a support group in the community. My first recollection of her is from when she showed up at the community group. We quickly became friends. After a year or so we had become best friends. Then we started to talk about getting married. We decided to see a marriage counselor to see if we were really compatible and to discuss with an expert how our illnesses (mine schizophrenia and hers schizoaffective disorder) would affect a possible marriage. The marriage counselor felt that we were one of the most compatible couples he had ever seen. On October 23, 2010, Kristen and I got married. As of this writing, we have been happily married for over nine years. This is my second marriage; my first ended in divorce in

January of 1980. This is Kristen's first marriage.

As you can see, I have lived a full and rewarding life despite the fact that I have suffered from schizophrenia for 35 years. Throughout those 35 years, I have been constantly reading about severe mental illnesses and educating myself about them. From 1997 to 2009 I was very active as a moderator of a website dedicated to supporting people who suffered from schizophrenia and their friends and family members. Since 2001, I have been a member and leader of a community support group for people with severe mental illness. Since 2003, I have been going to hospitals here in Columbus and talking to patients on psychiatric units about how to live and cope with having a severe mental illness. All of this has culminated in me writing this book to share the knowledge I have learned about living with a severe mental illness. I would like to dedicate this book to the mental health professionals who take the time to talk to and educate their patients about mental illness. It is my hope that whoever you are and whatever connection you have to severe mental illness, my book will help you understand how to cope and live with a severe mental illness.

Important Information About Diagnoses

You may have had many diagnoses during the length of your mental illness. Many of us have been told that our diagnosis was either schizophrenia, schizoaffective disorder, or bipolar disorder only to have it changed later. You may ask, "Why can't the doctors make up their minds what the diagnosis is?" Well, the answer is real simple. We do not have a diagnostic test for mental illness. If we measure your blood sugar and your blood sugar is 400, you have diabetes. A simple test and a simple answer. If we measure your blood pressure and it's 180 over 120, you've got high blood pressure. Again, something we can measure. But for mental illness, all we have to go on is what you say, what you do, what you tell us. We can't look inside your mind and see what's going on in there, so unless you tell us, we don't know. All the doctor does is make a list of what he thinks your symptoms are, then he goes to a book called the DSM-5 (or Diagnostic and Statistical Manual for Mental Illness Version 5) and looks up those symptoms. This book is a list of what symptoms go with what mental illness and the doctor tries to find the best match he can, and that becomes your diagnosis.

Different doctors may have different opinions. Sometimes symptoms change over the course of time. Sometimes the book itself changes. All these things can lead to changes in diagnosis. So it's important to realize that a diagnosis doesn't really do a whole lot for you. It's nice to have a label and to say I have such and such an illness, but what's important is that the treatment works and you're getting better. That's what you should be concerned about. Don't get too wrapped up around the diagnosis. But everyone should be encouraged to look up the DSM-5; it's usually found in the reference section of the library. You can read about your own diagnosis and then discuss it with your psychiatrist, who can answer any questions you may have. But again, the important thing is not the diagnosis—the important thing is that your treatment works and you're getting better. That's what you should be concerned about. Don't get too wrapped up around the diagnosis.

Regardless of what your current diagnosis is, it is important to learn as much as you can about whatever that diagnosis is. This is true whether your diagnosis is schizophrenia, schizoaffective disorder, bipolar disorder, cancer, diabetes, or heart disease. The more you know about whatever diagnosis you have, the better off you are in working with your treatment team. Knowledge is power.

It is also important to realize that there is no particular limit to how many different mental illnesses you can have, just like there is no limit to how many physical illnesses you can have. There are, however, some mental illness diagnoses that cannot both occur at the same time. Schizophrenia, schizoaffective disorder, bipolar disorder and depression are mutually exclusive diagnoses. If you have one of them, you cannot also have a second one at the same time.

What Is Psychosis?

The simplest way to explain psychosis is that it means a person is having hallucinations and delusions. When people are in psychosis, their thinking, emotions, and behavior are severely disturbed because they think the hallucinations and delusions they are experiencing are real.

Hallucinations are sensory experiences that only the person experiencing them has, while others around them do not experience them. The most common hallucination is auditory hallucinations. Auditory hallucinations are often referred to as hearing voices. It is important to realize, however, that as well as voices they can be any sound you can imagine hearing. Some people may hear doors slamming, bells ringing, telephones, and even music. Sometimes the auditory hallucinations can take the form of hearing a command to do something. Such auditory hallucinations are referred to as command hallucinations. The person may also have visual hallucinations, which, again, can be anything you can imagine seeing. The person may also experience hallucinations of taste, smell, or touch. Hallucinations can affect any of the five senses, and for the person experiencing them, it is often very difficult to tell the difference between hallucination and reality.

Delusions are fixed false beliefs that a person may have regardless of evidence to the contrary. Delusions may be grandiose in nature. For example, the person may think he is an important person, such as president of the United States or any other famous or important figure. Delusions regarding religion are also very common. The person may believe that he is a great prophet, the pope, the antichrist, or any other religious figure. Delusions can also be paranoid in nature. The person may think that the CIA or FBI is after them, that their phone is bugged, or that someone has implanted a computer chip in their brain to control or monitor them. There is no limit to what form a delusion can take. It is important to remember that to the person experiencing the delusion, it is absolutely real and factually true.

It is also important to realize that psychosis is a symptom, not a diagnosis. Psychosis is to a mental illness somewhat similar to what a fever is to a physical illness. In both cases they tell you that there is a problem, but they do not tell you what the problem is.

Schizophrenia

Schizophrenia is a serious brain disorder that has been described as one of the most debilitating and baffling mental illnesses. Schizophrenia is characterized by a dysfunction of the thought process affecting a person's ability to think clearly, to distinguish between what is real and what is imaginary, manage emotions, make decisions, relate to others, and to express normal emotions in social situations. Hallucinations, delusions, and withdrawal from the outside world also occur. There is a lot of variety within the condition. As with any medical condition, early and aggressive intervention/support will result in improved outcomes.

There are several stigmas (negative or unfair beliefs) about people who have schizophrenia. These stigmas include split personality, tendency towards violence, or personal weakness. These ideas about schizophrenia are myths. The majority of people with this illness do not pose a danger to others, but more often they are victims of violence.

What are the symptoms of schizophrenia?

- **Cognitive symptoms** – Trouble focusing or paying attention; disordered thinking and speech; difficulty with concentration or memory

- **Negative symptoms** – Negative symptoms are absent from a person's personality that normally should be present. Social avoidance, emotional withdrawal, apathy, emotionally unresponsive or flat affect, inability to express language, anhedonia (unable to experience pleasure), and lack of motivation, even for self-care (not laziness)

- **Positive Symptoms** – Positive symptoms, also referred to as psychotic symptoms, are things that are added to the person's experience that should not be there. It is important to realize that positive does not mean good symptoms. Psychosis is also a part of schizophrenia, and all schizophrenics have delusions and hallucinations. Auditory hallucinations are very common with schizophrenia.

Schizoaffective Disorder

Schizoaffective disorder is most easily viewed as having both schizophrenia and bipolar disorder at the same time, or having both schizophrenia and depression at the same time. Technically, you are supposed to have two weeks of psychotic symptoms without any mood disorder symptoms to receive this diagnosis, but often people are lumped into this diagnosis that don't quite fit the DSM criteria.

Bipolar Disorder

Bipolar Disorder is also known as manic depression. People with bipolar disorder go through periods where they are manic and may have very elevated mood, think they can do anything, engage in reckless behavior, and exercise poor judgment, and may talk very rapidly about constantly changing ideas they are thinking of. While manic, it is very common to sleep only 2 or 3 hours a night, or even not at all, but not feel tired. As well as periods of mania, they will also have periods of severe depression and may become suicidal. Some people with bipolar also become psychotic, most frequently when they are severely manic.

Depression

Everyone has some idea of what depression is. It is a period of very depressed mood. The person frequently has problems facing the world's pressures and may become very inactive. Depressed people often sleep excessively. Suicidal thinking is also quite common. It is also important to realize that this period of depressed mood has to last continuously for a period of two weeks or longer to be considered depression. Depression is not just being down for a day or two. It is also important to recognize that some people with depression do become psychotic.

Dual Diagnosis

Another issue with these diagnoses is that very frequently there is co-occurrence of abuse of alcohol, street drugs, or marijuana. When you have a problem of substance abuse in addition to a mental illness diagnosis, this is usually referred to as having a dual diagnosis in the United States. Many other English-speaking countries use the term "co-morbid disorder" for this instead. You may encounter that term if you travel to them or visit websites from those countries. Dual diagnosis is more difficult to treat than either problem by itself, but you can successfully treat it. The key is to work on both the substance abuse problem and the mental health problem at the same time. Working exclusively on one or the other problem frequently results in the neglected problem getting out of control.

Organizations such as Alcoholics Anonymous and Narcotics Anonymous may be very helpful in dealing with the substance part of these problems. One important caveat about these groups is that occasionally you may run into a member or a few members of these groups that do not believe you can be *"clean and sober"* if you are taking prescribed psychiatric medications. If you do run into this problem, tell the person or persons that they are not doctors and they do not know what they are talking about. You need your prescribed psychiatric medications to stay healthy. If you cannot resolve the problem with the individual or individuals, try a different chapter of the support organization. Most members of these groups do understand the difference between taking prescribed psychiatric meds and substance abuse.

Important Information About Medications

Almost all of us have tried many different medications over the course of our illness. Some may work well, but others either had side effects we couldn't tolerate or did not control our symptoms. That's very common with psychiatric medications. It's important to realize that they're all trial and error. No one knows in advance what a given psychiatric medication is going to do for you, not even the doctor. He makes an educated guess, but he doesn't know for sure.

And it's important to give these medications time to take effect. A lot of them take as long as three or four weeks for full effect, and the doctor probably won't make changes during that time unless it becomes totally obvious that it is not working or you're having severe side effects. All medications have side effects; even such common medications as aspirin and Tylenol have side effects. But the side effects of your psychiatric medications aren't as easy to deal with as those of aspirin and Tylenol. It is important to remember that what we are looking for is relief of our psychiatric symptoms. In order to get that relief, we may have to live with some side effects. Unfortunately, some of us must live with some symptoms in addition to the side effects. For example, some of us still hear voices occasionally, even though we take our medications as prescribed.

What we are really doing is a balancing act, looking for the most relief of symptoms paired with the lowest number and severity of side effects. That takes a lot of experimentation, including trial and error on the part of you and your doctor, to find what works best for you, because everyone is different. No two people respond to the same medication in exactly the same way. You are basically an individual experiment to find out what works for you. I would encourage you to keep working with your doctor until you do find a set of medications that does a good job of controlling your symptoms without causing too many side effects. But do be aware that it is trial and error, and it may take some time to find the right medications and dosage for you. Most of us have felt like guinea pigs at times as we try to find a medication regimen that works for us.

There has been a new development with medications. There's now a test to identify how medications are going to work for you. What they do is swab the inside of your cheek and collect some of your DNA. They send that DNA off to the laboratory to analyze. With what they find in your DNA, they can tell how your liver is going to metabolize most of the major psychiatric medications used today. Then what they do is send a list back to your doctor of which medications they think will work well for you and which medications they think will work poorly for you. He can use that list to decide what to try next with you. This is very new, and very promising, but we don't have a whole lot of experience with it yet. We're not sure how it's going to work out in the real world. But this is the closest we've ever been to taking the trial and error out of medication, so it's a really big deal. Again, what it does is tell your doctor how your liver is going to metabolize a medication, and that helps determine what dose should work for any given medication. It doesn't tell whether there will be bad side effects, and it doesn't tell whether it's a good drug for you. It just informs as to what dose should work, if this is the correct drug for you.

The Three Things That Are Most Likely to Cause A Relapse

There are three things that are responsible for the vast majority of all relapses of a mental illness. The first thing is a no-brainer. It's not taking your medications as prescribed. It's important to remember that mental illness is really chemical and physical problems in our brain, and that means that mental illnesses are *physical* illnesses. They are just as physical as diabetes, heart disease or cancer. Mental illnesses are physical illnesses.

Compare them to the type 1 diabetic. If you think about a type 1 diabetic for a moment, his pancreas does not produce insulin, so he has to take insulin shots to offset that. As long as he takes those shots as he's supposed to, he'll do well. If he stops taking his shots, he will become very sick in short order and die. Well, our medications are like the type 1 diabetic's. If we take them like we're supposed to, we'll do well. If we stop taking them, we'll very likely become sick in short order. We will not die as a direct result of not taking our medication, like a type 1 diabetic, but there are ways you can die as a result of not taking your psychiatric medication. Things like suicide or becoming delusional and thinking you can fly and jumping off the tenth floor of a building to prove it. There are ways you can die as a result of not taking your psychiatric medication.

There's another part of the type 1 diabetic's experience that is very important to us as well. That is that no matter how long the type 1 diabetic takes his insulin, it does not fix his pancreas. His pancreas is a problem for life. Our medications are the same way. They do not fix the problem in our brains. They only allow us to function as long as we take them. For almost all of us, it is medication for life because our mental illness is an illness for life. Just like the type 1 diabetic's pancreas is for life. That's the first thing that causes most relapses; not taking our medications as prescribed, and again, it's a no-brainer.

The second thing that causes most relapses is also a no-brainer. It's using alcohol, street drugs, or marijuana. Again, it's important to remember that our mental illness is really chemical and physical problems in our brain. If we start using substances like street drugs, alcohol, or marijuana, we're changing the chemical properties of our brains. It should be no surprise that this interferes with the normal function of our brains and the medications trying to help us cope with our mental illness. Again, street drugs, alcohol, and marijuana will likely cause a relapse in short order, and that's a no-brainer.

The third thing that causes relapses you may not be aware of. It may have caught you by surprise. You may still not have realized it's a problem. This third thing is stress. Stress can cause you to have more symptoms, it can cause you to need a higher dose of medication to control these symptoms, and it can cause an outright relapse. Stress can be a killer when you're dealing with a mental illness.

It's important to remember that stress is different for each and every one of us. We all get stressed by different things and in different ways and we all relieve our stress with different things and in different ways. We tend to think about things that are very bad as being stressful. Things such as getting fired or losing your job. That often is very stressful. But good things like getting married can be just as stressful as getting fired and can cause you just as big a problem with your mental illness. Again, stress is different for each and every one of us.

There's no way to live a stress-free life, so we have to find ways to deal with our stress. Some common things we use to reduce stress include exercise, meditation, listening to music, doing arts or crafts, reading, and journaling. It is also important to reduce the stress in your daily living. This usually includes getting on a regular sleep schedule and having a daily routine. Having structure in our lives is a great way to reduce our daily stress load. You've got to find the things that work for you because, again, stress is different for each and every one of us, both in what relieves it and what causes it. But do remember that stress can cause you to have more symptoms. It can cause you to need a higher dose of medication to control these symptoms, and it can cause an outright relapse. So watch out for stress.

These three things—not taking your medication as prescribed, using drugs, alcohol, or marijuana, and stress—cause the vast majority of all relapses. There are other things that can cause relapses, but those are the big three. If you think back over your life, one or more of those three things may have been a problem with one or more of your relapses.

Learning When to Ask for Help

There is something else that is very important in learning how to stay out of the hospital. That's to recognize when you're going downhill and when to ask for help before you wind up so far downhill that you end up back in the hospital. This is something that is different for each and every one of us. We all have different illnesses, different symptoms, and get sick in different ways. We all need to try and look back over our lives and identify those key things that tell us we're going downhill.

There are three common factors to look at to determine how we are doing. The first one of these things, and the most reliable indicator, is how we are sleeping at night. Anyone can have one sleepless night, but if we have two or three in a row, it is probably time to talk to our psychiatrist and get some help. People who have bipolar often sleep only two or three hours a night or not at all when they are becoming manic. Again, time to talk to your doctor. If you are sleeping all day, you may be depressed. You need to look at changes in what is normal for you.

Another thing to look at is symptoms that don't go away even though we are properly medicated. For example, some of us still hear voices occasionally. If they are becoming louder, more persistent, harder to ignore, or more of a problem, again, it's time to talk to our psychiatrist and get some help.

The third thing to look at is our overall thinking. When we start to become grandiose and paranoid and see all sorts of conspiracies and strange things going on in the world, it's time to talk to a psychiatrist and get some help. For some of us, we have two, three, maybe four days when we question whether this is all real. If we talk to our psychiatrist during that time and get a temporary medication increase until whatever has us stressed out goes away again, we will probably be okay. If we do not get that temporary medication increase, we will probably become fully psychotic and wind up back in the hospital and have to start all over again. Some people who are good at recognizing when they are going downhill have used this technique to stay out of the hospital for decades.

There's another thing you can do here, too, that is also very important. That is if you have a close friend or family member, somebody who knows you well and who sees you on a regular basis, they can sometimes tell when you're going downhill before you can yourself. And that can be a very big help, too. These friends and family members can help patients monitor changes in their behavior and mood. Again, it is very important to learn to recognize when you're going downhill and to get help before you wind up back in the hospital.

What Causes Severe Mental Illnesses

Most of us have wondered what causes mental illness. The truth is that we don't know the exact cause of any of the major mental illnesses, but we do know that genetics plays an important role in all of them. This is true of schizophrenia, schizoaffective, bipolar and depression. Genetics is important in all of these illnesses.

Now in the case of schizophrenia, about 1% of the population has schizophrenia regardless of family history, but it does often run in families. What we see is that if one parent has schizophrenia, the odds are about 10% that the child will, as opposed to 1% of the general population. If both parents have schizophrenia, the odds are about 50% that the child will. When we're looking at identical twins, there's something else interesting. If one of the twins has schizophrenia, the odds are only about 50% that the second one will as well. And that tells us something very important; that tells us that genetics is not the full story. There's something in the environment that causes this genetic predisposition to come out. We're not sure what all these environmental things are yet. It's sort of like cancer. We know a lot of things cause cancer to come out, and a lot of things seem to cause schizophrenia to come out.

Most of these things are things that are beyond our control. For example, problems during a mother's pregnancy, such as catching a virus while still in the womb. There's a parasite passed by cats, and it's believed that if the fetus contracts that parasite, it increases the risk of schizophrenia as an adult. Malnutrition on the part of the mother during her pregnancy has been linked as well. A lot of schizophrenics are born in the late winter or early spring. The best explanation we have for that is it appears that if the mother catches the flu during the second trimester in her pregnancy, the child will have a 3 to 7 times greater risk of developing schizophrenia than if the mother does not get the flu during the second trimester of her pregnancy. If her second trimester is during the late fall or early winter, when the flu is typically going around, that would explain the late winter/early spring births of people that are pre-disposed to schizophrenia.

There's another cause that first came up about 15 years ago and was kind of surprising when we first heard about it. This one is that the age of the father has a lot to do with whether the child develops schizophrenia. It turns out that if the father is 50 to 60 years old when he fathers a child, the child will have a 2 to 3 times greater risk for schizophrenia than if the father is 30 when he fathers a child. They're still doing research on that, but they have verified that statistic.

There's another cause for schizophrenia that has become prominent in the last 10 years, although evidence has been building for decades. This one is still controversial, and not everyone is willing to accept it, but there is getting to be quite a bit of scientific evidence to back this one up. And this is one that's under your control. It turns out that using marijuana seems to increase the risk of schizophrenia. We're not sure why this is yet, it's sort of like the link between smoking tobacco and lung cancer. If you do use marijuana, you're more likely to get schizophrenia, but we don't know exactly why.

It's never a good idea to use street drugs because street drugs often cause symptoms that look like a mental illness all on their own, and if you do have a mental illness, it usually makes the symptoms worse. So it's best to stay away from the street drugs. The only street drug we have a strong scientific link to today for causing schizophrenia is marijuana, but there are many other street drugs that are suspect as well. LSD, or acid, has been suspect for decades. We see a lot of people who use crystal meth or methamphetamines that go on to develop schizophrenia. PCP, Ecstasy, cocaine and many more are all suspect. It's important to remember that these street drugs are causing changes in your brain and that we don't know what the long-term effect of all those changes in your brain are. So again, the best thing to do is just stay away from street drugs entirely and have nothing to do with them.

We cannot point to any single thing and say this caused a person's mental illness. All we can do is say that certain things increase the risk. The cause of the illness is both genetic and environmental. If you have the genetic predisposition but don't get exposed to the environmental factor, you will not become ill. If you do not have the genetic predisposition, you will not develop illness even if you do get exposed to the environmental factor.

Although this explanation covers schizophrenia, there are similar links to environmental factors for the other diagnoses as well.

The Problem With Marijuana

You have undoubtedly heard a lot of positive press about marijuana (also known as cannabis). There are efforts underway to make recreational use of marijuana legal. There is also a lot of talk about medical marijuana. You may have noted that elsewhere in this book it was stated that marijuana is likely to cause a relapse. It is important to realize that for those of us with psychotic illnesses, marijuana is highly detrimental to our health.

In order to understand why marijuana is detrimental to us, you first need to understand how antipsychotic medications work. Every antipsychotic we have today works on the neurotransmitter dopamine. What the antipsychotics do is dampen down the dopamine activity in the brain, making it look like there is less dopamine available to the brain. This is how they control your hallucinations and delusions.

When you use marijuana, the THC also works on dopamine. What the marijuana does is increase the level of dopamine in the brain. This is what causes the high. That means marijuana works in the exact opposite direction of our antipsychotics. That is why it is so important for us to stay away from marijuana. You may also know that there are some forms of marijuana on the street today that are so potent they can cause psychotic symptoms in people that are not mentally ill. It is best just to avoid it entirely.

In the event that recreational use of marijuana becomes legal, you should keep in mind that just because something is legal does not mean it is good for you. After all, tobacco and alcohol are legal and we have tremendous problems with both of them.

With respect to medical marijuana, it is important to understand that there are at present two chemicals of great interest to medicine in marijuana. One is THC, which was addressed above. The second is cannabidiol, or CBD. There is some research indicating that although THC is very detrimental to people with psychotic illnesses, CBD may in fact be very helpful in treating psychosis. It is important to keep in mind that this is still being researched, and we do not know for sure if it is useful, and if it is, what dose is needed. Both CBD and THC are currently available in FDA-approved formulations that can be prescribed by a doctor. Medical marijuana also sometimes uses the whole plant as treatment even though we have no idea how the many other chemicals in marijuana affect us. At this point the only thing we can say for sure is that for any doctor to prescribe a medical marijuana product containing THC to someone who is known to have a psychotic illness would probably constitute malpractice.

Violence and Mental Illness

There's a very common stereotype that mentally ill people are violent and dangerous. Hollywood has done a lot to perpetuate that stereotype. The Norman Bates character from Alfred Hitchcock's movie *Psycho* is probably the classic example. He's stabbing people in the shower and running around doing all kinds of crazy things. Well, unfortunately, there are a few people with mental illness who are violent and dangerous, but they're actually few and far between. Most people with mental illness are not violent and dangerous towards others. In fact, they're much more likely to be the victims of a violent crime rather than commit one, because they are usually easy targets. If you watch your local news on television, you will see a lot of violent crimes. Most of those violent crimes are being committed by people who are not mentally ill; they're just violent and dangerous people.

When we do look for someone with a mental illness who is going to become violent and dangerous, there are three things to look for: Look for someone who is not taking his medication, someone who is abusing alcohol or drugs (and that does include marijuana), and someone who has a history of violence. Each of those three things is a problem in and of itself, and they are all three contributing factors. When you see all three together, that's someone you really want to watch out for, as they're extremely likely to become dangerous.

We have a perfect example right here in Columbus, Ohio of how the stereotype gets perpetuated. You may remember the Ohio highway sniper in 2004 who was out shooting at cars on Interstate 270. When they caught up with him, his diagnosis was schizophrenia, and that made all the headlines in all the newspapers. Everyone said schizophrenics are violent and dangerous people. It hurt everyone dealing with a mental illness. When we look a little closer, he was schizophrenic, but he was not taking his medication, he was abusing alcohol, and he had a history of violence. So he was someone you could expect to become violent, and he did.

Currently, there are more than a million people living here in Franklin County. Since about 1% of the population has schizophrenia, that means that there are more than 10,000 schizophrenics here in Franklin County as well. Obviously, we don't have 10,000 people shooting at cars on 270. Most of those people are just trying to live as normal a life as possible and get along as best they can, in spite of their mental illness. There are indeed a few that are dangerous, but they are few and far between. The thing to look out for is someone who is not taking his medication, someone who is also using alcohol or drugs, including marijuana, and someone who has a history of violence. When you see those three things together, watch out.

If you are someone who's been violent, you cannot change your past. You will have to live with having been violent. But you do have control over whether or not you're taking your medications, and you do have control of whether or not you're using alcohol, drugs, or marijuana. So you still have control of two of the three things that indicate you're most likely to become violent and dangerous again. Your future, your destiny, is still in your own hands.

Coping With Symptoms That Don't Go Away

For those of us suffering from a psychotic illness, a major part of learning to cope is realizing that we can never again be 100% sure what reality is. For many of us, some residual symptoms still remain even though we are properly medicated. Following is a recommended strategy for coping with this that I developed.

I still hear voices occasionally even though I am properly medicated. Learning to tell when something is or isn't real is something I've worked on over the years. I drew up my own strategy for how I cope with hearing voices. What I do is I divide the things I experience up into three buckets. The first bucket is those things that I'm pretty sure are real, that are actually happening and are real-world stuff. The second bucket is those things that I'm pretty sure are hallucinations and delusions and not actually happening. And I have a third bucket of things that I'm just not sure about.

I put things into those three buckets based on my past experiences as to what's real and what's not real. I've learned over the years that something said directly to me face-to-face is usually real, I very seldom hallucinate that. So that's probably going in the bucket of real stuff. If it's something whispered down the corridor, down the hallway, those are things I often hallucinate. And then I look at the content of what I've just heard and ask myself, does this make sense? Would the person really be saying that, or would the person know that, and does it make sense? And if the answer is no, it does not make sense, then it goes in the bucket of hallucinations and delusions and I just forget about it. If it is something that I don't know for sure about, it goes into that third bucket of things I'm just not sure about. I leave things there until I do get information that will allow me to put them into one of the other two categories. Sometimes I never do get that information, and that can be very frustrating. It just kind of festers to not know what's real. But I've learned that acting on things that are not real can have very severe consequences for me, so I choose to just sit there and be frustrated rather than act on things that may not be real. And that's how I've learned to cope with my voices, and that's my strategy.

I think it's important for everyone to try to develop a strategy for how to cope with their hallucinations and recognize what's real and what's not real so they can better cope with the real world. You are going to make mistakes, I do occasionally, but it's important to try and develop a technique to help you decide what's real and what's not real so that you can better cope with the real world.

What Is Stigma?

Stigma is a word that is used often in conjunction with talking about mental illness. Stigma is a politically correct way to talk about the prejudice and discrimination that people with mental illness face. Some of us believe that the word stigma should not be used because it does not carry the force and understanding of the issue that the words prejudice and discrimination convey. The word stigma allows the issue to be discussed without the negative connotations and outright anger that the words prejudice and discrimination carry. Some people would like to see the word stigma taken out of our vocabulary entirely so that people will realize what the true issue is.

Stigma, just like discrimination and prejudice, is usually based on ignorance and unfamiliarity with mental illness. Stigma is when people buy into the negative stereotypes about mental illness that are so prevalent in our culture, just like the negative stereotypes about race and cultural background which are often so roundly condemned in our culture today, even though they still exist.

Stigma presents itself in many ways. Stigma can come from those around us. These are people that believe that if you are mentally ill, you are likely to become violent. The vast majority of us are not violent. Many believe that if you are mentally ill, your thinking and intelligence are impaired. Which, again, is another myth. It is also very common to believe that you are incapable of taking care of yourself, live on your own, or be financially self-sufficient. Again, this is totally untrue and another myth, though it has a small kernel of truth in that a small number of us are indeed severely incapacitated by our illness. Others of us live full, productive and relatively normal lives. Some of us hold very demanding and prominent jobs and do well despite being mentally ill.

These beliefs are widespread in our society, and most if not all of us have encountered these beliefs and attitudes. They come at us from the community, sometimes from family members, and even sometimes from ourselves when we buy into these beliefs. Perhaps the worst source of stigma, however, comes from the mental health profession itself. There are mental health professionals that do not believe that someone with schizophrenia can function highly and hold a demanding job. Some mental health professionals will not even tell you what your diagnosis is. The mental health professionals do a poor job of education as to what mental illness is and how to treat it. Many of us may know what our diagnosis is but have a very poor understanding of what that diagnosis entails or how it is treated because our treatment team does not value the education of the patient.

Compare this situation with someone receiving a diagnosis of type 2 diabetes. If you are diagnosed with schizophrenia today, not only do you receive very little education, but you may not even be told your diagnosis. Sometimes all you get is a prescription for a bottle of pills and an appointment to return at a later date. When someone is diagnosed with type 2 diabetes, not only will you be told your diagnosis, you will receive all sorts of additional help in the form of handouts about what it is and how it is treated. You are also likely to be told about support groups and receive counseling from a nutritionist on how to change your diet. For many, there will be recommendations of weight loss and classes on diet and nutrition. This difference in treatment is a clear indication of the prejudice and discrimination from the mental health profession against its patients. The mental health profession does not seem to understand that education of the patient on his or her mental illness is in the best interest of the patient, just like with type 2 diabetes. Granted, there are some mentally ill patients who will not cooperate with education and treatment, but the medical profession finds that some people with type 2 diabetes also will not cooperate with education and treatment. This is clear evidence of prejudice and discrimination by the mental health professionals towards their patients. As in other areas as well, there are many mental health professionals who do not buy into the prejudice and discrimination and do an excellent job. Until the accepted standard of care for mental illness includes education of the patient and hopefully his or her family as well, we will not have a stigma-free mental health profession.

When Should I Disclose My Diagnosis?

The decision as to when and to whom to disclose your diagnosis is a very personal decision. There are no right or wrong answers, and what we choose to do is entirely up to us.

With respect to friends and family, it is usually wise to disclose your diagnosis. If they don't know what you have, they will not be able to properly support you and help you deal with your illness. You should also be prepared to educate them about your diagnosis, as most people do not have a very good understanding of what the mental illnesses actually are, what their symptoms are, and how to best treat them. Do be aware, however, that sometimes a friend or family member will have nothing to do with you after they find out what your diagnosis is. This is usually a result of ignorance about the mental illness.

Work is a very different story. Mental illnesses are covered by the ADA (the Americans with Disabilities Act) and it is illegal to discriminate against someone based on their mental illness. The ADA also says that the employer must make reasonable accommodations if the disabled person needs them in order to perform the job. It is important to remember the term "reasonable" is used. You still must be able to do the job and perform satisfactorily in it, and the employer is not required to completely revamp the job especially for you. An example of reasonable accommodation might be having a desk in a low traffic area, as noisy, busy places are stressful to you. To get reasonable accommodation, you must discuss and disclose your disability to the Human Resources Department. The HR department will determine if the accommodation is reasonable and inform your supervisor of the accommodation if it is deemed reasonable. The HR department is obligated to keep your diagnosis secret if you so desire. This is important, as if you wish to say you were discriminated against under the ADA, the burden of proof is on you. If you have disclosed to your supervisor and/or your co-workers, it may be very difficult to prove that you did not get that pay raise or promotion as a result of them knowing your diagnosis. Sometimes it can also work to your advantage to disclose the diagnosis if you are in a good work environment. This is a critical decision for you to make, and you must remember that once you disclose, you cannot un-disclose. There are people who have been treated very well after disclosing their diagnosis, and people who have actually won discrimination lawsuits against employers after disclosing their diagnosis. Again, there are no right or wrong answers, and the decision is totally up to you as to whether or not to disclose.

Sexual Side Effects of Antipsychotics

Although they are rare, there are side effects of antipsychotics that do affect us sexually. These sexual side effects are almost always caused by the antipsychotic artificially raising the levels of the hormone prolactin in the patient. Blood tests can check for this problem and may be used to verify that the sexual side effect is a result of raised prolactin levels. In all cases, these side effects indicate a need to switch to a different antipsychotic. The sexual side effects usually present themselves in the first 2 to 3 months of being on an antipsychotic that causes this problem in the patient. As with other side effects, we have no way to know if a given patient will experience these side effects or not when starting on a new antipsychotic. The sexual side effects will go away once the medication is changed to a different antipsychotic. It is important to tell your doctor immediately if you are experiencing any of these side effects. There is no need to be embarrassed when talking to your mental health professional about these side effects. Your mental health professional needs to know about these side effects so that they can be addressed promptly.

Side Effects That Can Occur in Both Women and Men

❖ The most common side effect in both women and men is a loss of interest in sex.

❖ Both women and men may experience a discharge of fluid from their breasts.

❖ Both men and women may not be able to achieve orgasm

Side Effects That Can Occur in Women

❖ Women may not have their period.

Side Effects That Can Occur in Men

❖ There may be difficulty in getting or maintaining an erection.

❖ There may be breast enlargement in men.

❖ There is a side effect known as retrograde ejaculation. This means that the sperm flows into the bladder instead of out the penis.

Are Newer Antipsychotics Better?

We have all seen advertisements for things that say newer is better and more improved. This same sales pitch is often used by pharmaceutical companies to make you want to use their product. Unfortunately, when it comes to antipsychotics, the actual picture as to whether newer is better is very complicated and ultimately depends on what you, the patient, value in terms of likely side effects for a given antipsychotic.

Today we frequently divide all antipsychotics into one of two groupings. The first grouping is referred to by three different labels. These three labels are old antipsychotics, typical antipsychotics, and first-generation antipsychotics. The second grouping also has three different labels. These three labels are new antipsychotics, atypical antipsychotics, and second-generation antipsychotics. Many of the first-generation antipsychotics have been around since the 1950s and 1960s. The second-generation antipsychotics first began appearing in the 1990s and there are still new ones being FDA approved today.

The first-generation antipsychotics are more likely to cause movement-related side effects such as EPS (extrapyramidal side effects) and Tardive Dyskinesia. These side effects have been apparent since the introduction of these meds. EPS is the stiffness, shakiness, and jerky muscle movements, among others. Tardive Dyskinesia is an uncontrollable twitching or movement of a group of muscles. This is most commonly seen in the form of twitching lips, or the tongue slipping in and out of the mouth, but it can affect other parts of the body as well. EPS is often very uncomfortable and sometimes very scary but can easily be treated by side effect medications such as Cogentin or by switching to a different medication. Tardive Dyskinesia is a disfiguring side effect that is viewed very negatively and is not so easily treated as EPS. Tardive Dyskinesia is often a cause to try a different medication, but Tardive Dyskinesia is sometimes permanent. Since 2017, we have had two FDA-approved medications to treat Tardive Dyskinesia.

When the second-generation antipsychotics arrived on the scene in the 1990s, they were touted by all the pharmaceutical companies as having much fewer side effects than the first-generation antipsychotics. This was based on drug trials, which, in almost all cases, was a comparison between the first-generation antipsychotic Haldol and the second-generation antipsychotic which was the subject of the trial. In most of the studies, the dose of Haldol selected for the trial was actually much higher than is commonly used in routine practice. Haldol is noted for causing EPS, and with the higher than normal dose selected for the study, EPS was extremely likely. Also, these studies usually did not give Cogentin or any other side effect medication for EPS to the patients taking Haldol. As we know, today the second-generation antipsychotics are much less likely to cause EPS, so because of the design of the drug trials, it seemed obvious that the second-generation antipsychotics had fewer side effects. At this time, it was also believed that second generation antipsychotics did not cause Tardive Dyskinesia. The result of all this was a widespread belief that second-generation antipsychotics were far superior to first generation antipsychotics. This belief was spread far and wide by drug reps, and most psychiatrists accepted this as fact. By the early 2000s, people were claiming that use of an old antipsychotic should be considered malpractice.

By 2004, it had become obvious that there were problems with the new antipsychotics. The first problem to surface was that the new antipsychotics often caused excessive weight gain, among other problems. A short time later, the FDA required a warning for all second-generation antipsychotics that stated they were likely to cause type 2 diabetes. Within the next couple of years, the problem with the second-generation antipsychotics had a name. It was metabolic syndrome. Metabolic syndrome is a cluster of physical changes that include weight gain, high cholesterol, high triglycerides, and type 2 diabetes. There were other problems associated with this as well, such as high blood pressure and cardiovascular problems.

In 2005, a milestone in drug trials was completed. This was a study known as CATIE, or Conventional Antipsychotic Trials of Intervention Effectiveness. This study, run by NIMH, the National Institute of Mental Health, compared outcomes of patients treated with several antipsychotics in a clinical setting. The antipsychotics used included several second-generation antipsychotics and one first generation antipsychotic. The outcome of this study turned the psychiatric world upside down. The first-generation antipsychotic used in the test (Trilafon) performed just as well as the second-generation antipsychotics. Trilafon had the highest rate of discontinuation for the side effect of EPS, which was no surprise. The antipsychotic which had the highest rate of discontinuation due to side effects was in fact the second-generation antipsychotic Zyprexa, primarily due to excessive weight gain. This test also showed in a different phase that the only antipsychotic that was more likely to work for the patient than any other was Clozaril. Clozaril is a second-generation antipsychotic which has a serious problem with a side effect called agranulocytosis. This means the patient's white blood cell count drops dramatically and the patient can die from an infection. Clozaril is safe to use because any patient taking it must have frequent blood tests to ensure that agranulocytosis is not occurring. If agranulocytosis is occurring, stopping use of Clozaril immediately will prevent any serious complications. In all other respects, Clozaril is just like other second-generation antipsychotics in that it often causes metabolic syndrome.

Since the completion of the CATIE study, it has become apparent that the pharmaceutical company line that the second-generation antipsychotics had fewer side effects was not true. The first- and second-generation antipsychotics simply have different side effects that are most likely. Today we know that you can get EPS and Tardive Dyskinesia from any antipsychotic. You can also get metabolic syndrome from any antipsychotic. It is simply a matter of which is most likely. For the first-generation antipsychotics, EPS and Tardive Dyskinesia are more likely. For the second-generation antipsychotics, metabolic syndrome is more likely. It is also important to realize that there is no way to predict what side effects any given patient will have on any given antipsychotic until that patient tries it. You as the patient have a say in what antipsychotic you take. In cooperation with your doctor you can decide if you are more comfortable with a higher risk of one side effect than another. Tardive Dyskinesia is a very serious side effect that some people simply don't want to take a higher risk in developing. For others, the metabolic syndrome is viewed as a more serious side effect because it can shorten your life. The choice as to first generation or second-generation antipsychotic is between you and your doctor. One additional point to consider in your choice of antipsychotic is price. First generation antipsychotics are typically much less expensive than second generation antipsychotics.

It should also be pointed out that the CATIE study was done only in patients with schizophrenia. It is true that the second-generation antipsychotics also affect serotonin as well as the dopamine that the first-generation antipsychotics have an effect on. It is often said that due to the serotonin effects, the second-generation antipsychotics are better for bipolar disorder than the first-generation antipsychotics. It is true that most second-generation antipsychotics are FDA-approved for both schizophrenia and bipolar disorder, whereas no first-generation antipsychotic is FDA-approved for bipolar disorder.

There is, however, a good reason why no first-generation antipsychotic is approved for bipolar disorder. When each second-generation antipsychotic was approved for bipolar disorder, it was still under patent. When the pharmaceutical company spent the large amount of money required to conduct the studies to get that approval for bipolar disorder, it could then market for a second diagnosis and make a lot more money because of the fact that it was under patent and only they could sell that antipsychotic. All first-generation antipsychotics are no longer under patent. As a result, the pharmaceutical company making the generic drug cannot reap any significant additional profits by having that antipsychotic approved for bipolar disorder. Because of this economic reality, the makers of the generic first-generation antipsychotics have no incentive to pay for the extensive studies needed to obtain approval to treat bipolar disorder. What is desperately needed is a study on patients with Bipolar Disorder similar to CATIE to see if there is indeed any significant difference in outcome between first- and second-generation antipsychotics in bipolar disorder. Due to the economics of this, the only entity which might spend the money for such testing is the government. It should also be noted that first generation antipsychotics were commonly used to treat bipolar disorder for many years prior to the second-generation antipsychotics coming on the market.

Several second-generation antipsychotics have also been approved to treat depression. The situation here is very similar to the above discussion on bipolar disorder except that first-generation antipsychotics were not commonly used to treat depression without psychosis prior to the arrival of second-generation antipsychotics. Because there is no economic reason for generic drug makers to pay for testing their product for depression, it is quite unlikely to happen unless government funds the study.

Forced Treatment

Most people dealing with a severe mental illness have the common experience of being psychotic. Unfortunately, each experience of psychosis is different. There is no way to say in advance what form or directions any particular individual's psychotic symptoms will take. When we are psychotic, our actions are totally unpredictable. I have never been a danger to self or others when I was psychotic. It is important to remember that I was trained as a soldier. I am an expert with small arms, trained in hand-to-hand combat, and have extensive knowledge of explosives. All of those skills are still available to me when I am psychotic. I firmly believe that I could be extremely dangerous when psychotic because of those skills.

It is important for all of us that we take our meds as prescribed and work with our treatment team to avoid becoming psychotic again. Unfortunately, even when you are doing everything right, it is still possible to slip back into psychosis without realizing it. When that happens, depending upon exactly what form our delusions take, we may stop cooperating with our treatment and refuse treatment. When this happens, we frequently believe that there is nothing wrong with us and that there is no reason for us to be detained and medicated. We will also usually not recognize that there is a very real potential that we could become a danger to self or others. It is readily available information that after 10 years, approximately 10% of schizophrenics are dead due to either suicide or accidental death. Delusional thinking often plays a major role in these deaths.

There is a lot of controversy about what society should do with us when we are psychotic and refusing treatment. Most of this controversy is because many people do not understand the nature of psychosis and the fact that people who are psychotic are completely out of touch with reality. There is a similar issue with when we are too drunk to drive. Someone who has been drinking heavily may not realize that his judgment and reactions are seriously impaired. If that person is talking about driving, most people will agree that taking the keys away from that person is in the best interest of both the individual and the public at large.

Today, we have a standard procedure for police officers to do a breath analysis or a blood alcohol test to determine when someone is driving drunk. Before these things were available, the officer had to do a visual assessment of how impaired a person was. This included such things as walking a straight line, could a person touch his nose with his eyes closed, and many more subjective tests. Psychiatrists of today are very much in the position of the police officer because we have no medical tests to establish when one is psychotic or to what degree. The psychiatrist has to rely on his own subjective assessment of how grounded a person is in reality. Although this subjective assessment is known to be unreliable, just like the subjective tests for drunk driving that police officers used to do, it is the only thing we have available today.

When, in the best judgment of the psychiatrist, we are so psychotic that we are likely to become a danger to self or others, he will ask us to admit ourselves to the hospital for evaluation. If we refuse to go voluntarily, the psychiatrist has the option of placing us in the hospital for a 72-hour hold. During this time, the hospital staff will evaluate us in more detail than the psychiatrist gets to do in his initial interview. If at any time during that period it is decided that we are in fact OK, the hospital can release us. If at the end of that 72-hour hold we are deemed to still need hospitalization, we will be asked once again to stay voluntarily. If we choose not to do so, the psychiatrist will initiate a hearing before a judge to have us committed involuntarily to the hospital. At this hearing, we will be represented by an attorney, two psychiatrists will testify as to what they think our state of mental health is, and then the judge will make a decision as to whether or not we will continue to be held in the hospital against our will.

Unfortunately, at no point during this process is there any way to ensure that we are taking our meds in order to return us to sanity. After we have been committed to the hospital by the judge, the psychiatrist has to initiate a second court hearing to get permission to forcibly medicate us if we will not take medication on our own when asked to do so. This second court hearing is usually successful because the judge will not be able to end the commitment order unless we do take medication and cooperate with the treatment team. Unfortunately, there is no way to know that we will continue to take medication when released, and some people cycle into and out of hospitals continually as a result.

Despite mountains of evidence to the contrary, some people refuse to believe that we are potentially dangerous simply because we are psychotic. This is, in fact, a serious problem with our legal system. Under present law, a psychotic person has a legal right to be homeless, live under a bridge, and eat out of a garbage can so long as he cannot be proven to be a danger to self or others and is breaking no laws. It is hard to believe that people can consider this situation to be morally and ethically acceptable, but many do.

To show how bad the current system is, one needs only to look at one current and very troubling statistic. Currently in the state of Ohio, if you have a diagnosis of schizophrenia, schizoaffective disorder, or bipolar disorder, you are four times more likely to be in a jail or prison than a hospital. Most of those mentally ill people in jail or prison were not taking their medications and frequently were abusing alcohol, marijuana, or street drugs when they committed whatever crime got them arrested. Most reasonable people would agree that appropriate treatment in a hospital is much better than the often terrible treatment mentally ill people receive in a jail or prison. It should also be obvious that although it is highly undesirable to force people to accept treatment, failing to do so has serious negative implications for both the individual and society at large.

What Is Recovery?

What does it mean to be in recovery? Many people have many different ideas. Some people think that unless you are an executive in a Fortune 500 company, you are not a success. Others think that if you are working at a part-time job, like being a cashier in supermarket, you are in recovery. Still others think that being a volunteer at an animal shelter is to be in recovery. In my view, recovery could be all of those things and many more. It is my view that recovery means that you are doing the best you possibly can and living the most fulfilling life that is possible for you, each and every day.

For all of us, the first and most important step in our recovery is to cooperate with our treatment team and follow their advice. Beyond that, what we do is limited only by our personal abilities and limitations. When embarking on the road to recovery, we must first take inventory of our abilities and limitations in a realistic fashion. If we are overly optimistic in that inventory, we will find that we are unable to fulfill the lofty goals we have set for ourselves. If we are overly pessimistic about that inventory, we will find that we have neither challenged ourselves nor realized our full potential. It is also important to reassess those abilities and limitations periodically, as they may change over the course of our mental illness.

What we can accomplish today may not be the same as what we could accomplish last month or next year. It is important to remember that recovery is a personal thing. We should not compare ourselves to others. There will always be people who do better or worse than us. We should not look enviously at people who do better than us, we should instead congratulate them on their good fortune. Likewise, we should not look down on those who cannot do as well as us, but instead offer them help and encouragement in their efforts to do better.

For almost everyone, if your abilities and limitations allow you to work at a full-time paid job, you are almost always better off if you do so. This will allow you the positive effects and self-esteem of being self-supporting, having a purpose in your life, being socially engaged with your coworkers, and having the positive benefits of being paid for what you do. Before embarking on getting a paid job, be sure to check out the ramifications of going off disability if you are on it. Social Security can be a very problematic agency to work with if you do not follow their rules and guidelines to the letter.

Perhaps you need a little additional education to get that dream job. Going back to school to get that additional education can be very rewarding. Most schools have special accommodations for students with disabilities, and you probably qualify. Remember, however, that if you need a lot of special accommodation in school, you may not meet the requirements for that dream job. As always, you need to evaluate what your abilities and limitations are before making career decisions. Going back to school without any clear career goals in mind is usually not a good idea for anything except a GED or high school diploma.

For those of us who cannot work at a full-time paid job, many of us can work at a part-time job for pay. This carries with it all of the positive benefits of a full-time paid job except that your paycheck will not be as large. Also, if you are on disability, you can keep most of your benefits from being on disability provided you follow the rules and guidelines of Social Security. Get an expert to help you deal with Social Security, as they are very unforgiving of people who make mistakes.

For those of us who cannot work at a paid job, most of us are capable of working as a volunteer somewhere for a few hours a week. As a volunteer, you frequently can set your own hours, pick work you like to do, and even choose what kind of stress level you will have to deal with. Volunteer work is just as beneficial as paid work except you are not earning pay. Many of us find volunteer work highly rewarding and satisfying. Also, if you do well at a volunteer job, you will often be able to use that job for references if you decide to try out for a paid job later. It is highly recommended that if you are planning on returning to paid work, you should work as a volunteer for a while first. Volunteer work allows you to build your coping skills and learn how to interact with people in a safe and non-threatening environment. If you do poorly at a volunteer job, it does not have to go on your record, and you can easily start over at another volunteer job and hopefully have a better outcome.

Unfortunately for a few of us, even volunteer work is too stressful and beyond our abilities. If you are one of these people, you should strive to be a good citizen. This means cleaning up after yourself, doing the laundry, doing the dishes, mowing the lawn, and helping out your neighbors and friends when they need help. Be the best helper and friend you can be to those in your life.

For all of us, another important aspect of recovery is doing our best to stay out of the hospital by following the advice of our treatment team. It is important to remember that sometimes when things get out of control, despite our best efforts, we may need to return to the hospital for a period of time to re-stabilize. This should not be looked on as a failure but rather as a learning opportunity to help prevent the next hospitalization. Remember that recovery is simply doing the best you can each and every day, and that what that best is can change.

What Is Anosognosia?

Anosognosia was first studied in stroke patients. In some stroke patients, the person would be unable to move an arm due to the stroke but was unaware of this and thought his arm was moving normally. Studies of these patients showed that there was stroke damage to a particular part of the frontal lobes of the brain that appears to be involved in self-reflection. In schizophrenia, schizoaffective disorder, and bipolar disorder, the illness sometimes causes damage to this same part of the brain. These individuals are physically incapable of recognizing that they are mentally ill no matter how obvious their mental illness may be to anyone else around them. It is very hard to treat mentally ill people with this condition because they see no problem with themselves and therefore do not see any need to take medications. This becomes extremely pronounced when the person is actually psychotic, and most patients who are psychotic have some version of this problem. When the person is placed on medication, often forced on them, the anosognosia often diminishes to an extent. For many, however, the condition itself never goes away completely. The world's leading expert on anosognosia is a psychologist named Xavier Amador. He has written a book called *I Am Not Sick, I Don't*

Need Help! on the subject. This book is highly recommended to people working with someone who has anosognosia.

It is important to recognize that anosognosia is not being in denial. Being in denial is a psychological issue where the person does not believe they are ill but do have the capacity to realize they are. Denial and anosognosia look very similar and it is hard to differentiate between them. Even mental health professionals sometimes are not sure which issue is presenting itself in a given patient.

If you are a person who has anosognosia, you may be totally unaware that you are having symptoms and problems caused by your mental illness. If you find that you are being hospitalized repeatedly for a mental illness you do not think you have, you may well suffer from anosognosia. It is highly recommended that you listen to people you trust and cooperate with treatment. You will often find that your life improves dramatically if you listen to them and cooperate with treatment, even though you may think the problem exists with the world and not you.

A Day in My Life

Darrell Herrmann was diagnosed with schizophrenia in 1984 at age 30 while serving as a captain in the United States Army. His specialties were field artillery and nuclear weapons. Due to schizophrenia, Darrell retired from the army. He went back to college and got a computer science degree and began working as a professional computer programmer. He worked successfully at this profession from January 1987 to November 2004 when the stress of working became too much for him. Darrell has not had a psychotic break since 1991. The following is what a typical day in his life was like while working as a computer programmer in 1998 at Bank One, which is now Chase.

The alarm is ringing. I get up groggily to shut it off. I ask myself for the millionth time when I can't sleep, is it better to take the sleeping pill and be hung over or just be sleepy from lack of sleep? I take my morning medications. I shower and shave. I get dressed. No breakfast, I can't eat for an hour after meds. It is off to work, the daily commute.

I arrive at my desk at 10 till 8. I check my voicemail. The boss wants to see me *now*! He has a new hot priority project. It is an ad-hoc report that one of the vice presidents has suddenly expressed interest in. It is Tuesday; he wants it no later than Friday. Discussing it with the boss shows that it will be a fairly simple program with a sort. It needs to read in the journal transactions for the company and spit out a report showing the detail transactions with a total for each account. I go back to my desk and start writing Cobol Code. It quickly becomes obvious that the report will not fit across a single page of paper because there is too much information on a line. A quick call to the business analyst reveals that they must have all the info. I suggest two detail lines for each transaction. He balks but eventually realizes there is no better solution. I return to my coding.

By 10:30 I have a sample report to show my boss. He approves the report and we call the business analyst. He says it looks fine, but he wants a different header on the report. Also, he feels that any account with less than $5,000 is not enough to worry about and he doesn't want to see them on the report.

While this discussion is going on, I become aware of a whispered conversation about me coming from the adjacent cube. It quickly becomes obvious that this conversation couldn't be real. It must be my voices. I have lost my place in the conversation. It ends. I get my boss to summarize the new requirements so I can cover for being distracted by my voices. Neither he nor my coworkers know that I am schizophrenic. It quickly becomes obvious that once again we have given the client exactly what he asked for, but naturally, this isn't what he wanted.

I head back to my cube to write a new set of programs. Due to the new requirements, it will take two much more complex programs to produce the report. On my way back, a woman I have seen but don't know says, "Hello, Darrell." How did she know my name?

What does she know about me? Stop! You don't have time for paranoia; there is work to be done.

11:30. Lunch time, and I have to make my monthly visit to my doctor today. In the car, a quick drive to McDonald's drive-thru. Eat a sandwich while I complete my drive to the doctor's. As usual, he is on time. We spend 15 minutes discussing how things are going and he writes me new prescriptions. I make an appointment for next month. I drive back to the office. I am back at my desk at 12:40 pm. We only get an hour for lunch. Did anybody notice I was late?

Back to the programming. The phone rings. It is production control. A job has gone down. A quick check shows that it is a server problem. I call the support center to open a ticket to fix the server. Back to the programming. I hear another whispered conversation down the hall. Ignore it; they can't be talking about me.

By 4:00 I have the programs written and debugged. Back to the boss. He looks it over and says it looks good. Call the business analyst. He looks it over and approves. He wants the same report for all companies in group one and can he have it tomorrow. We agree. My boss says, "Thanks! You are my best programmer and fast, too!"

Five o'clock and quitting time. Time to think about supper. One of the nice things about being a programmer is that I am well paid. I feel like celebrating a bit because I did a tough job well. I eat out almost every night because I hate cooking. Tonight, I want a filet mignon with mushrooms and a baked potato. After a good meal at the steakhouse, it is back to my nice two-bedroom townhouse.

I walk into the living room and turn on my stereo. I put on the Rippingtons. I sit down at my PC and check AOL for email. Then it is off to schizophrenia.com to see what is new. Hmmm, another kid doing a term paper that wants all the answers handed to him. An interesting and informative post by the site psychiatrist. After I finish the posts, it is time to check on the chat rooms. Hmmm, no one is here yet. I go in anyway and wait for someone to show.

"Hi friend, how's the music business?"

"Hello friend2, what is new with you?"

Hmmm, a new friend, friend3.

"Hello friend3, welcome to the best schizophrenia site in the world. How can we help you?"

Friend3 says her son was recently diagnosed with schizophrenia and after three months in the hospital he is coming home. He is 15. She is concerned about schooling for him. She wrote a local special school that specializes in mental patients. She asked them how many of their students go on to college. She was told to be realistic and to realize her son's potential. She wants to know what is possible. He wants to be a computer programmer writing computer games. What can she tell her son?

"Tell him that you met a professional programmer who is schizophrenic and works full time. He got his degree in computer science after being diagnosed as schizophrenic."

Stigma Against Schizophrenics by Mental Health Professionals

Speech Prepared for Concord Counseling Center by Darrell E. Herrmann for 14 September 2017

I would like to thank you all for giving me the chance to address this group on the issue of stigma against schizophrenics by mental health professionals. I would also like to thank Mary Kay Ansley for inviting me and setting up this opportunity to speak to you. I am sure that some of you know me well, and others have just heard stories about me, and some probably have no clue as to who I am. Therefore, I would like to open this speech by telling you a little about my background.

In 1984 I was a captain in the United States Army. My specialties were field artillery and nuclear weapons. I began to believe that I had been drugged with an experimental drug as part of a secret conspiracy to produce super soldiers. I believed that this was why I couldn't sleep at night, couldn't cope with my work, and generally was just falling apart. Because I thought I had been drugged, I decided to go to the army hospital and ask them for help with this. They quickly realized that I was becoming delusional and psychotic and I wound up on a military psychiatric ward. At that point, it was obvious that I needed to make a career change, as psychosis and nuclear weapons just don't go together. I decided to go back to college and become a computer programmer. In January of 1985 I began studying full time for my computer science degree. In December of 1986, two years later, I completed my degree. In January of 1987 I began working full time as a computer programmer and did that successfully for almost 18 years until November of 2004 when the stress finally became too much for me and I went on disability.

I moved to Columbus in 1995 for a job at Bank One, which is now Chase. In July of 1997 I bought my first PC and got on the internet. I quickly found the website schizophrenia.com and got involved with it. This was the first opportunity I had to talk to someone with schizophrenia outside of a psych ward. When you are walking down the street, people don't have a sign on them saying "I have schizophrenia," so you don't know when you meet someone who has it because they are not about to tell you they have it. (During my entire time from leaving the army in 1984 to about two months before I left my last paid job, I disclosed my diagnosis to no one in my workplace outside of medical professionals.) In spring 2001, I came across a listing for a Schizophrenics Anonymous (SA) group on the website for Mental Health America of Franklin County (MHAFC). I decided to give it a try and join. I made friends with people there and found that for the first time I had a place to talk openly about my illness, symptoms, and related issues in face-to-face conversations. I found this very helpful. In spring 2002, the psych ward at Doctor's West contacted our group about having speakers from our group come in and talk to their patients on Friday afternoons. A group of three women agreed to do this. In Fall 2002, the psych ward at Riverside also approached our group about having speakers come in and talk to their patients on Friday evenings. As this was after my work hours, I was very interested in helping with this effort. I had misgivings about word that I was doing this getting back to my workplace at Chemical Abstracts but decided that if I did meet people who knew me while speaking at Riverside, they would probably understand and be discreet about my diagnosis. I began doing groups at Riverside in January of 2003. After I went on disability, I approached MHAFC about doing groups on other psych wards here in Columbus. MHAFC was able to get me invites to begin doing groups at other hospitals here in Columbus. I am currently doing 8 hospital groups each week. In 2016 I saw more than 3700 people in these groups. As of today, I have spoken to more than 2500 people in these groups in 2017.

I have done many things as a mental health advocate since being on disability, but the one other thing I think is noteworthy is that I was responsible for beginning a project between MHAFC, NAMI of Franklin County, and The Ohio Psychiatric Physicians Association to produce a set of fact sheets on 7 diagnoses that we considered serious mental illnesses. These fact sheets were designed to provide basic information about each diagnosis and also to provide additional resources such as support groups, reputable websites, and good books to start educating the reader about each diagnosis. My goal was to give each psychiatrist in Columbus a book containing copies of each fact sheet and encourage them to copy those fact sheets and give them out to their patients as appropriate. I personally wrote the first draft of each fact sheet prior to turning them over to the three organizations involved in this project for their editing. In the fall of 2006, I helped prepare over 200 binders with these fact sheets for those psychiatrists and assisted the Ohio Psychiatric Physicians Association to distribute them to all Columbus psychiatrists. In January of 2007, I was nominated by Laura Moskow Sigal, the executive director of

MHAFC, for a Jefferson Award to recognize my contributions to the community. I was selected to receive a Jefferson Award and was recognized as one of five Jefferson Award recipients by the *Columbus Dispatch* and Channel 10 WBNS. A news article about all five award recipients appeared in the *Columbus Dispatch*, and WBNS ran a three-minute story about each of us individually several times during their news broadcasts in April.

Enough about me, I am here to talk to you about stigma from mental health professionals. One thing that really drove home to me the tremendous amount of stigma in the mental health profession against their patients is the reaction those fact sheets I mentioned above got from the psychiatrists. Some (including my own psychiatrist) were very glad to receive them and made excellent use of them. Unfortunately, I also found out that many psychiatrists were uncomfortable or unwilling to talk to their patients about the information in those fact sheets and would not use them. This unwillingness to discuss these issues openly is something I have personal and family experience with. My father became psychotic in 1959 when I was four years old. He was hospitalized and received both insulin shock therapy and Electro Convulsive Therapy. He always credited this with bringing him back into reality. I always attributed his recovery to the little blue pill called stelazine, which he took. My father did well with his illness and successfully ran the family farm for many years after the death of my grandfather. My father died in 2004. During his entire lifetime, no medical professional ever told him what his diagnosis was. My family believes that his diagnosis probably was schizophrenia, just like mine.

When I became psychotic in 1984, no one in the military psych ward would tell me what my diagnosis was. I knew that I had a legal right to read my own medical records, so I demanded to read them. I found out that my diagnosis was schizophreniform disorder, which meant exactly nothing to me. I received no help with education about mental illness in general, or mine in particular, from the military medical system. When they released me from the hospital, I went to the library and tried to find my diagnosis in psychology textbooks. To this day I have never seen a psychology textbook that listed schizophreniform disorder, but I did find information on schizophrenia and realized that what I had experienced matched the description of that diagnosis. When I returned to college in January 1985, I spent a lot of time in the college library trying to find out all I could about my diagnosis. Unfortunately, as you may know, the bulk of writing and research on schizophrenia at that time was based on psychoanalysis. I quickly dismissed this stuff as garbage because it did not fit my case at all. In the summer of 1985, I came across a newly released book on schizophrenia called *Surviving Schizophrenia* by E. Fuller Torrey M.D. This was the first book I had ever found that made sense of my experiences and clearly spelled out what schizophrenia was and how best to treat it. The education I received from this book set my feet firmly on the road to recovery. Had I not found that book and all the helpful information in it, I do not believe I would be here today talking to you.

When someone receives a diagnosis of type 2 diabetes, they usually get all sorts of help in the form of handouts, appointments with dieticians, and classes on how to cope and live well with their illness and even information for support groups. To this day, if you are diagnosed with schizophrenia, you are likely not to be told your diagnosis. You are extremely unlikely to get any education or handouts on the diagnosis. Your treatment team probably does not know how to contact or even consider support groups to be of value to you. In fact, all you are likely to get is a prescription for medication and an appointment to come back in a month. Although this is the accepted standard for care for schizophrenia, if this standard were applied to any "physical ailment" (I firmly believe that schizophrenia is a physical ailment, although it is often considered not to be one), that standard of care would be considered totally unethical and unacceptable. In fact, most mental health professionals in my experience cannot even explain in simple understandable language what schizophrenia is to their patients. As a result of this, I have developed a short speech I use to explain what schizophrenia is.

I often find that mental health professionals themselves have a serious bias against patients with schizophrenia and believe that they are incapable of living a relatively normal life. This manifests itself in two ways. The first way is that if you are, in fact, doing relatively well, then you obviously cannot have schizophrenia. My last psychotic break was in 1991 while I was living and working in Cincinnati. My psychiatrist at that time did not believe I could be schizophrenic because I was working very successfully as a computer programmer, and schizophrenics simply couldn't do that. He changed my diagnosis to bipolar disorder and started me on mood stabilizers. Initially it was lithium, but he later added Tegretol as well while continuing me on an antipsychotic. As time went on he decided that bipolar really didn't fit me so he changed my diagnosis to schizoaffective disorder but left me on the same medications. In 1994, I relocated to Little Rock, Arkansas and the diagnosis of schizoaffective disorder stuck with me. In 1995 I moved here to Columbus and again the diagnosis of schizoaffective disorder stuck with me. My new psychiatrist ordered blood tests which showed that my liver function was not good. She decided to stop the Tegretol but was worried that I might relapse. After several months with no relapse, I was forced to find a different psychiatrist because she left her practice. My new psychiatrist did a very thorough and effective intake interview. He asked me whether or not I had ever been manic. I told him that I did not think I had ever had any experience of what he described as mania. He told me then that he suspected I was in fact schizophrenic, as the army had originally diagnosed me many years before. After much discussion with this new psychiatrist, we decided to stop the lithium in 1997. Since that time, the only psych med I have taken is my antipsychotic Trilafon. Although I have occasionally had symptoms of psychosis that required time away from work and occasionally temporary increases of my antipsychotic, I have not relapsed in all those years. I consider this to be pretty good evidence that schizophrenia is, in fact, the right diagnosis for me.

The second way that the pervasive stigma against schizophrenics manifests itself is in the low expectations mental health professionals have for schizophrenics. They are sometimes quite open about those low expectations. For example, when MHAFC arranged to have me start doing groups at one hospital here in Columbus, I was told quite openly by a hospital administrator that they put their most difficult and severe cases in one particular unit and that these were almost always schizophrenics. Because I was doing groups about Schizophrenics Anonymous, it would only apply to schizophrenics, and since almost all the schizophrenics were on that one unit, I was told that I would only be doing groups on that one unit. At that time, no other hospital in Columbus that I was working with segregated their patients in that manner. In the other hospitals, the patients were assigned at random into wherever there was an open bed. It was my observation that on the segregated unit, the patients were indeed acting out, very symptomatic, and hard to deal with. Discipline and patient behavior on that unit were indeed quite terrible. In the other hospitals I worked with, you did occasionally see a patient acting out and very symptomatic, but this was not common. It is my opinion that by segregating their patients, the staff had very low expectations of the patients, there was no peer pressure to behave, and, as a result, the patients ran amok. While this segregation may have made it easier for the staff on the other units, on the "severe cases unit," life was absolutely miserable for both the staff and patients. I firmly believe that low expectations for this unit is what caused that unit to be so miserable.

I would like to leave you with one last depiction of mental health professional stigma against schizophrenics. Three years ago at the MHAFC annual get-together and awards presentation, one of the facilitators for an S.A. group received an award for her outstanding work with the group during a turbulent period when a few individuals were making, as it was put, very bad choices for themselves. She had done an outstanding job of dealing with those individuals. After the ceremony, I and two other members of the SA group were standing with our facilitator and congratulating her on her well-deserved award. A gentleman that none of us knew came up to our little group and congratulated the facilitator on her award. He added that he knew it was very difficult to work with schizophrenics and he admired her for doing that. He knew nothing about the difficulties that the facilitator had dealt with, which had nothing to do with the fact that the people were schizophrenics, and it apparently had never occurred to him that three schizophrenics might be standing there with their facilitator congratulating her on her well-deserved award.

Four Useful Websites

www.nami.org : National website for the National Alliance On Mental Illness

www.mhanational.org : National website for Mental Health America

www.curesz.org : Website for the CURESZ Foundation. This foundation is small but impressive. They advocate for more use of Clozapine, long-acting injections, and treatment for Tardive Dyskinesia. They have several excellent YouTube videos on schizophrenia and various issues related to it, as well as treatments.

www.ProjectDailyPages.org : Project Daily Pages is a nonprofit organization dedicated to helping those with mental illness live more stable, more productive, and more successful lives by developing routines and using a daily planner.